Determination and Dedication Building Strong Faith As A Young Man

Joshua Rhoades

Published by Joshua Paul Rhoades, 2024.

DETERMINATION AND DEDICATION BUILDING STRONG FAITH AS A YOUNG MAN

First edition. September 20, 2024.

Copyright © 2024 Joshua Rhoades.

ISBN: 979-8227580696

Written by Joshua Rhoades.

Also by Joshua Rhoades

Courage Under Fire: David's Stand On The Battlefield
Jonah's Journey: Voices Of Redemption And Lessons In Obedience
The Furnace Of Faith: 12 Principles From The Heat Of Faith
Whispers of Hope: Inspiring Stories of Men's Prayers In Scripture
Frontier Legends: The Oregon Dream
Elijah: A Beacon Of Boldness
HOOK, LINE & SAVIOUR - Faith Reflections from Fishing
Driven By Faith: Motor Racing Inspired Christian Life
30 Day Devotional - Bold and Strong- Coffee Devotions for a Courageous
Christian Walk
Authentic Christianity: The Heart of Old Time Religion
Consider The Ant - God's Tiny Preachers
Flee Fornication: The Plea For Purity
Renewed Hope- How to Find Encouragement in God
Sounding The Call - The Voice of Conviction
The Altar - Where Heaven Meets Earth
The Bible's Battlefields- Timeless Lessons from Ancient Wars
The Sacred Art of Silence - How Silence Speaks in Scripture
Under Fire- The Sanctity of the Traditional Biblical Home
Who Is on the Lord's Side? A Call to Righteousness
What Is Truth? - From Skepticism to Submission
First and Goal- Faith and Football Fundamentals
From Dugout to Devotion- Spiritual Lessons from Baseball
Par for the Course- Faith and Fairways
The Believer's Pace- Tools for Running Life's Marathon
The Immutable Fortress- Security in God's Unchanging Nature
Biblical Bravery
Deer Stands and Devotions: A Hunter's Walk with God

Jesus Knows- Our Hearts, Our Responsibility

Restoration - Setting The Bone

Spiritual 911- God's Word for Life's Emergency's

The Freedom of Forgiveness

The Jezebel Effect - Ancient Manipulations Modern Lessons

The Shout That Stopped The Saviour

The Time Machine Chronicles: Old Testament Characters

Anchored In Truth Exploring The Depths of Psalm 119

Biblical Counsel on Anger

Proverbs' Portraits The Men God Mentions

Stumbling in the Dark - The Dangers of Alcohol

Guarding the Wicket Protecting Your Faith and Game

The Champion's Faith - Wrestling and Achieving Spiritual Victory

Scriptural Commands for Modern Times Living God's Word Today Volume 1

Scriptural Commands for Modern Times Living God's Word Today Volume 2

Scriptural Commands for Modern Times Living God's Word TodayVolume3

The Greatest Gift

A Christmas Journey of Faith

Daughter Of The King: Embracing Your Identity In Christ

Determination and Dedication Building Strong Faith As A Young Man

Dedication

To the young man who is seeking to live for God, this dedication is for you. In a world full of distractions, temptations, and countless voices pulling you in different directions, you have made a choice—a choice that many your age often overlook or shy away from. You've decided to pursue something deeper, something lasting. You've chosen to live for God. This choice, though not easy, is one of the most powerful and rewarding decisions you will ever make. It speaks to the desire in your heart to live a life that honors the One who created you and to walk a path that leads to true purpose and fulfillment.

Living for God is not always simple, and there will be times when you feel unsure of the next step or how to navigate the challenges before you. But I want you to know that God sees your heart. He knows your desire to serve Him, and He is ready to guide you every step of the way. He doesn't expect you to have all the answers right now, and He's not asking you to be perfect. What He desires is your heart—your willingness to follow Him, trust Him, and learn from Him. Psalm 119:9 asks, "Wherewithal shall a young man cleanse his way? by taking heed thereto according to thy word." This verse reminds us that the key to living a life for God is found in His Word. The more you seek Him through Scripture, the clearer your path will become.

There will be moments when you feel alone in your journey, especially when it seems like others around you are living for themselves, chasing after temporary pleasures or worldly success. In those moments, it's important to remember that you are never alone. God is with you, guiding you, strengthening you, and providing everything you need to live a life that pleases Him. He has a plan and a purpose for your life, and He's inviting you to walk with Him on this incredible journey of faith.

One of the most crucial aspects of living for God is consistency. It's easy to feel excited and passionate at the beginning of your journey, but living for God is not just about a one-time decision. It's about the daily choices you make—the small acts of obedience, the moments of quiet prayer, the time spent in His Word, and the way you treat others. Proverbs 3:5-6 encourages us to "Trust in the LORD with all thine heart; and lean not unto thine own understanding. In all thy ways acknowledge him, and he shall direct thy paths." When you rely on

God, seek His guidance, and trust Him, He will direct your path, even when you can't see the full picture.

As you continue on this path of living for God, I encourage you to stay determined. There will be trials, challenges, and temptations that try to pull you away, but stay the course. God is faithful, and He promises to be with you through every challenge. Dedicate yourself to growing in faith, to deepening your relationship with God, and to serving Him with all your heart. You are not walking this journey alone. You have the support of your brothers and sisters in Christ, the wisdom of God's Word, and most importantly, the presence of the Holy Spirit guiding you.

Remember, your faith in the Lord Jesus Christ will be your foundation. It will shape the man you become and the impact you have on the world around you. God has called you for a purpose, and He is equipping you with everything you need to fulfill that purpose. Stay strong, stay committed, and know that the life you're building—one rooted in faith, determination, and dedication—will lead to lasting fulfillment and a deeper relationship with God. Keep pressing forward with determination and dedication to the glory and honor of Almighty God!

Introduction

As a young man in today's world, you are surrounded by countless challenges, temptations, and pressures. Society tells you to focus on material success, popularity, and personal achievement. It constantly pushes you to be someone who fits into its mold. But deep down, you know there's something more important to pursue—something greater than what the world offers. That something is a strong, unshakable faith in God.

Faith is not something that comes easily. It takes time, effort, and intentionality to build a solid foundation. It requires both determination and dedication. Determination to stand firm in the face of opposition and temptation, and dedication to consistently seek after God, even when it feels tough. Strong faith doesn't happen by accident. It grows through the choices you make each day and the habits you form over time.

This book, "Determination and Dedication: Building Strong Faith as a Young Man", is designed to help you cultivate that kind of faith. It's not about being perfect or having all the answers. Instead, it's about learning how to develop the character and spiritual discipline needed to live a life that honors God in a world that often pulls you in the opposite direction.

Throughout this book, you'll explore what it means to live with a sense of determination, focusing on God's purpose for your life. Determination is about standing firm when others may waver, staying true to your beliefs even when it's not popular, and having the courage to face adversity without backing down. In a world where distractions are endless, determination keeps your eyes fixed on what matters most: your relationship with God and your commitment to living a life that reflects His love and truth.

But determination alone isn't enough. You also need dedication—the daily decision to put God first in all you do. Dedication is about developing spiritual habits that strengthen your faith. This includes setting aside time for prayer, diving into God's Word, and making choices that align with His will. Dedication means that even when it's inconvenient, you're willing to prioritize your walk with God. This kind of dedication builds spiritual resilience, helping you to persevere through difficult seasons and grow deeper in your faith.

Living a life of faith as a young man is not always easy. There will be times when you feel discouraged, tempted to give up, or wonder if it's even worth it. But with determination and dedication, you can stand strong. The faith you build now will be a firm foundation for the rest of your life, helping you navigate the ups and downs with wisdom and strength that only come from God.

In "Determination and Dedication – Building Faith As A Young Man", we will explore practical, biblical principles that will guide you as you strive to strengthen your faith. You'll discover how to overcome obstacles, develop strong habits, and grow in your relationship with God. By learning to rely on God's strength, you'll be able to face life's challenges with confidence, knowing that your faith is grounded in the One who never fails.

So, are you ready to take the next step in building your faith? Are you willing to commit to the process of growing spiritually, even when it's hard? This journey will require effort, persistence, and heart, but it will also be one of the most rewarding things you'll ever do. It's time to embrace your calling as a young man of faith—determined, dedicated, and strong in the Lord. Let's begin this journey together.

Chapter 1 - Dedication

Dedication is a crucial part of building strong faith as a young man. To fully commit your life to God's service means that you are ready to give your whole self—your mind, your heart, your body, and your spirit—to the Lord. This kind of dedication is not something that happens overnight, but it begins with a choice. In Romans 12:1-2, Paul urges believers to present their bodies as a living sacrifice, holy and acceptable unto God, which is our reasonable service. This means that your life should be like a gift offered to God, where everything you do is done with the purpose of glorifying Him. Your dedication to God involves making a decision to live in a way that pleases Him, not just sometimes but all the time. It's a choice to be different from the world, to not conform to the patterns and expectations that society places on you, but to be transformed by the renewing of your mind through God's Word. In making this dedication, you are committing to think differently, act differently, and live differently because your life now belongs to Jesus Christ, the King of Kings. This decision will impact every part of your life—how you talk, how you treat others, the choices you make, and even the dreams and goals you set for your future. God wants to use your life in ways that you might not even imagine, but it starts with your dedication. In Colossians 3:23, we are reminded that whatever we do, we should do it heartily, as unto the Lord, and not unto men. This means that your dedication to God should be wholehearted. When you work, whether it's in school, at a job, or in your personal projects, you should always be giving your best effort because you are ultimately working for God, not just for people. This mindset shifts how you approach even the most mundane tasks because you begin to see everything as an opportunity to honor God. Dedication is not just about what you do in church or in your Bible study; it's about how you live your life every day. When you wake up in the morning, you can ask yourself, "How can I dedicate this day to God? How can I use my time, my energy, and my talents to serve Him?" This kind of dedication will require discipline. You'll need to make time for prayer, Bible reading, and worship, even when you're busy or tired. You'll have to resist temptations that come your way, and sometimes, you'll have to say no to things that seem fun or easy because they don't line up with the way God wants you to live. Dedication also means staying committed to your faith when things get tough. There will be times when you feel like giving up, when it seems easier to go along with what everyone else is doing instead of standing firm in your faith. But when you are truly dedicated to God, you will keep pressing forward, trusting that God is with you and that He will give you the strength to stay faithful. It's important to remember that dedication is not about being perfect. None of us are perfect, and we all make mistakes. But being dedicated means that even when you mess up, you come back to God, ask for forgiveness, and keep moving forward. It's about having a heart that desires to please God above all else. As a young man, your dedication to God can set the course for your entire life. It will shape the kind of person you become, the kind of relationships you build, and the kind of legacy you leave behind. You have the opportunity to make a lasting impact in the world, but it starts with being dedicated to living for God. This means being willing to surrender your own plans and desires to God's will, trusting that His plans for you are good and that He knows what is best for your life. One of the most powerful examples of dedication in the Bible is the life of Daniel. As a young man, Daniel was taken captive to a foreign land, where he was surrounded by people who didn't believe in the same God he did. But Daniel remained dedicated to God, even when it would have been easier to give in to the pressure around him. He prayed to God faithfully, even when it meant risking his life, and God honored his dedication by protecting him and using him to influence kings and nations. Daniel's story shows us that when we are dedicated to God, He can use us in amazing ways, even when we face difficult circumstances. Another example of dedication is the life of the Apostle Paul. Before Paul became a follower of Jesus, he was dedicated to persecuting Christians, but when he encountered Jesus on the road to Damascus, everything changed. Paul's dedication shifted from his own agenda to God's mission, and he spent the rest of his life preaching the gospel, even when it meant enduring persecution, imprisonment, and suffering. Paul's dedication to God's service was so strong that he was willing to give up everything for the sake of Christ. In Philippians 3:7-8, Paul says, "But what things were gain to me, those I counted loss for Christ. Yea doubtless, and I count all things but loss for the excellency of the knowledge of Christ Jesus my Lord: for whom I have suffered the loss of all things, and do count them but dung, that I may win Christ." Paul's life reminds us that true dedication to God is about being willing to sacrifice our own desires, ambitions, and even comfort for the sake of knowing and serving Jesus. Dedication also involves a commitment to serving others. Jesus said in Mark 10:45 that He came not to be served, but to serve, and to give His life as a ransom for many. As a young man, you are called to follow Jesus' example by dedicating your life to serving others. This could mean helping out at home, being a good friend, volunteering at church, or looking for ways to make a difference in your community. When you dedicate yourself to serving others, you are showing the love of Christ in a practical way, and you are fulfilling God's purpose for your life. In Matthew 25:40, Jesus says, "Verily I say unto you, Inasmuch as ye have done it unto one of the least of these my brethren, ye have done it unto me." Your dedication to God is demonstrated in how you treat others, especially those who are in need. As you continue to grow in your faith, you'll discover that dedication to God brings incredible blessings. When you dedicate your life to Him, you'll experience a deeper sense of peace, knowing that you are living according to His will. You'll find joy in serving Him and in seeing how He works through you to bless others. And most importantly, you'll grow closer to God, as your relationship with Him becomes the foundation of everything you do. It's important to understand that dedication is not something you do just once—it's a daily decision. Every day, you have the opportunity to dedicate your life to God anew. This means waking up with a mindset that says, "God, today I choose to live for You. I choose to follow Your will, to serve You with all my heart, and to trust You with my life." This kind of dedication will require perseverance, especially when things don't go the way you expect or when you face challenges that test your faith. But remember that God is faithful, and He will honor your dedication. In James 1:12, we are reminded that "Blessed is the man that endureth temptation: for when he is tried, he shall receive the crown of life, which the Lord hath promised to them that love him." Your dedication to God is not in vain. God sees your heart, and He is pleased when you choose to live for Him, even when it's difficult. As you dedicate yourself to God, you'll also need to stay connected to Him through prayer and reading His Word. In Joshua 1:8, God tells Joshua, "This book of the law shall not depart out of thy mouth; but thou shalt meditate therein day and night, that thou mayest observe to do according to all that is written therein: for then thou shalt make thy way prosperous, and then thou shalt have good success." Spending time in God's Word will strengthen your dedication and help you stay focused on His will for your life. Prayer is also essential to your dedication, as it allows you to communicate with God, seek His guidance, and find the strength you need to remain faithful. In 1 Thessalonians 5:17, Paul encourages us to "pray without ceasing." This doesn't mean that you have to be on your knees all day, but it does mean that you should maintain a constant attitude of prayer, always being mindful of God's presence and seeking His help in everything you do. Finally, your dedication to God will inspire others. As you live out your faith with determination and dedication, people around you will see the difference in your life. They'll notice the way you handle challenges, the way you treat others, and the way you live with purpose. Your dedication can be a powerful witness to those who don't yet know Jesus, and it can encourage other believers to stay strong in their faith. In Matthew 5:16, Jesus tells us, "Let your light so shine before men, that they may see your good works, and glorify your Father which is in heaven." Your dedication to God is not just about you—it's about shining the light of Christ in a world that desperately needs to see Him. So, as you commit your life fully to God's service, remember that dedication is a journey, not a destination. It's a daily choice to live for God, to serve others, and to trust Him with every part of your life. It will require sacrifice, discipline, and perseverance, but the rewards are far greater than anything the world can offer. You have the opportunity to make a lasting impact for God's kingdom, and it all starts with your dedication to Him. Whether you're just starting out on your faith journey or you've been following Jesus for a while, now is the time to renew your dedication to God. Ask Him to help you stay committed, to give you the strength to overcome temptation, and to guide you as you seek to live a life that honors Him. With determination and dedication, you can build a strong faith that will carry you through whatever challenges life throws your way. Trust in the Lord, lean on His promises, and dedicate yourself fully to His service. God has amazing plans for your life, and He will be with you every step of the way as you walk in faith and dedication to Him.

Chapter 2 - Discipline

Discipline is an essential part of building strong faith as a young man, and it plays a key role in your spiritual walk and daily life. Discipline means having self-control and the ability to say no to the things that tempt you, distract you, or lead you away from God's purpose for your life. It is the practice of training yourself to do what is right, even when it is difficult or when no one else is watching. In 1 Corinthians 9:27, the Apostle Paul talks about the importance of discipline when he says, "But I keep under my body, and bring it into subjection." What Paul means is that he works hard to control his body and its desires, making sure that his actions and decisions are aligned with God's will. This is a powerful example of how discipline helps you stay on the right path, keeping your mind and heart focused on God and His purposes for your life. Discipline in your spiritual life begins with your relationship with God. It means setting aside time each day to read your Bible, to pray, and to listen to what God is telling you. In a world full of distractions, it can be hard to stay consistent in these practices, but discipline is what keeps you grounded. Just like an athlete trains his body to stay fit and strong, you need to train your spiritual life by spending time with God, learning His Word, and growing in your understanding of who He is. This takes dedication and determination, but it is through this discipline that your faith will grow stronger. 2 Timothy 1:7 reminds us that "God hath not given us the spirit of fear; but of power, and of love, and of a sound mind." This verse teaches us that God has equipped us with the strength and self-control we need to live disciplined lives. A sound mind means that we have the ability to think clearly, make wise choices, and stay focused on God's will for our lives. Discipline is not just about avoiding bad things; it's about making the right decisions that will bring you closer to God and help you grow in your faith. It's about saying yes to the things that will strengthen your relationship with God and help you become the man He created you to be. There will be times when discipline feels hard. You may be tempted to follow the crowd, to take the easy way out, or to do things that feel good in the moment but lead you away from God's path. This is when discipline becomes most important. It's in those moments that you must remember who you are and who you belong to. You are a child of God, called to live a life that honors Him. Discipline is what helps you stay true to that calling, even when it's not easy. When you practice discipline, you are training yourself to resist temptation and to make choices that reflect your faith. It's not always fun or comfortable, but it's necessary for building a strong foundation of faith that will carry you through life's challenges. Discipline also helps you in your daily life, beyond your spiritual walk. Whether it's in school, sports, work, or relationships, discipline is what sets you apart as someone who is reliable, responsible, and committed. It's about doing your best, even when you don't feel like it, and pushing yourself to achieve your goals. Discipline teaches you to manage your time well, to stay focused on your priorities, and to keep moving forward, even when things get tough. One area where discipline is especially important is in controlling your thoughts and actions. What you think about and how you respond to situations can have a big impact on your spiritual growth. The Bible teaches us to take every thought captive and make it obedient to Christ (2 Corinthians 10:5). This means being intentional about what you allow into your mind and heart. Discipline helps you to filter out the things that are harmful to your faith, like negative influences, bad habits, or sinful desires, and instead focus on things that are pure, lovely, and true. Practicing discipline also means learning to control your emotions. It's easy to let anger, frustration, or sadness get the best of you, but discipline teaches you to pause, reflect, and respond in a way that honors God. Instead of reacting out of emotion, you can choose to respond with kindness, patience, and love. This takes practice, but over time, discipline will help you develop a Christlike character that reflects God's love to those around you. Another important aspect of discipline is being accountable to others. Surrounding yourself with people who support your faith and encourage you to stay disciplined is crucial. Whether it's a friend, mentor, or family member, having someone to hold you accountable can help you stay on track when you're struggling to maintain discipline on your own. When you have someone to check in with, pray with, and encourage you, it becomes easier to stay committed to your spiritual growth. God has given you the ability to live a disciplined life, but it's up to you to put it into practice. Discipline requires effort, persistence, and a willingness to make sacrifices. But the rewards are worth it. As you grow in discipline, you will find that your faith becomes stronger, your relationship with God deepens, and you are better equipped to handle the challenges that come your way. Living a disciplined life also brings peace and stability. When you know that you are living according to God's will and making choices that honor Him, you can rest in the assurance that you are on the right path. Discipline helps you avoid the chaos and confusion that come from living without direction, and instead gives you a clear sense of purpose and focus. As you continue to build your faith, remember that discipline is not about being perfect. It's about progress. There will be times when you stumble, make mistakes, or feel like giving up. But discipline is what helps you get back up, learn from your mistakes, and keep moving forward. It's not about doing everything right all the time, but about consistently striving to live a life that pleases God. The journey of building strong faith as a young man is not always easy, but it's one that will shape you into the person God created you to be. Discipline is the tool that will help you stay on course, resist the distractions and temptations of the world, and grow in your relationship with God. As you exercise discipline in your spiritual walk and daily life, you will see the fruit of your efforts in the form of stronger faith, deeper relationships, and a life that reflects the love and character of Christ. So, take up the challenge of discipline, knowing that God has given you the power, love, and sound mind you need to succeed. Be determined to stay committed to your faith, to live a life of purpose, and to honor God in all that you do. With discipline as your guide, you can build a strong foundation of faith that will carry you through every season of life, helping you to grow closer to God and become the man He has called you to be.

Chapter 3 - Devotion

Devotion is the cornerstone of building strong faith as a young man, and it involves having an unwavering love and commitment to God through prayer and Bible study. True devotion goes beyond just attending church on Sundays or reading a few Bible verses now and then. It's about living every day in a way that reflects your love for God and your desire to grow closer to Him. It's about making time for God in your daily life, allowing His Word to guide your actions, decisions, and thoughts. Devotion is not just something you do out of duty, but it is a reflection of your relationship with the Lord. In Joshua 1:8, God gives Joshua clear instructions about devotion to His Word: "This book of the law shall not depart out of thy mouth; but thou shalt meditate therein day and night, that thou mayest observe to do according to all that is written therein: for then thou shalt make thy way prosperous, and then thou shalt have good success." This verse is a powerful reminder that God's Word is meant to be an integral part of our lives. We are to meditate on it day and night, meaning that we should be constantly thinking about and applying God's truths to our lives. As a young man, developing this kind of devotion to God's Word will be key to building a strong and enduring faith. When you make the decision to be devoted to God, you are choosing to align your life with His will. You are saying, "God, I want You to be the most important part of my life. I want to live in a way that honors You, and I want to know You more." This kind of devotion requires consistency. Just like a strong friendship or relationship requires time and attention, your relationship with God requires you to spend time with Him regularly. Prayer and Bible study are two of the most important ways to cultivate your devotion to God. In prayer, you have the opportunity to speak directly to God, to share your heart, your concerns, your joys, and your struggles. Prayer is not just about asking God for things, but it's about building intimacy with Him, listening to His voice, and aligning your will with His. Devotion through prayer means you're not just coming to God in times of need, but you're making prayer a constant part of your life, talking to Him throughout the day and seeking His guidance in every situation. In Psalm 119:105, the psalmist says, "Thy word is a lamp unto my feet, and a light unto my path." This verse beautifully illustrates the role that

God's Word plays in our lives. Just like a lamp guides us through the darkness, God's Word guides us through the challenges, decisions, and uncertainties of life. Devotion to the Word of God means that you are committed to letting His truths direct your steps. When you make a habit of studying the Bible, you will find that it brings clarity to confusing situations, comfort in times of difficulty, and wisdom for daily decisions. The more you immerse yourself in Scripture, the more you will see how relevant and powerful it is for every aspect of your life. As a young man, your devotion to God's Word will help you build a foundation of faith that can withstand the storms of life. There will be times when you face challenges, temptations, and pressures that test your faith. In those moments, your devotion to God's Word will be what keeps you grounded. When you've spent time meditating on Scripture and storing God's truths in your heart, you will have the strength and wisdom you need to stand firm in your faith. Devotion to God is also about obedience. In Joshua 1:8, God tells Joshua to meditate on His Word so that he may "observe to do according to all that is written therein." It's not enough to just read the Bible or know what it says; true devotion means putting God's Word into practice. It means living out your faith in your daily life, in the way you treat others, in the decisions you make, and in the values you uphold. Devotion requires that you not only hear God's Word but that you are also a doer of the Word (James 1:22). This kind of devotion will set you apart as a young man who is serious about following Christ. As you grow in your devotion to God, you will begin to see the fruit of that devotion in your life. Your relationship with God will deepen, and you will experience His presence in ways that bring peace, joy, and purpose. Devotion to God brings a sense of fulfillment that nothing in this world can offer. It gives you a sense of direction and meaning, knowing that your life is part of God's bigger plan. It also strengthens your faith, giving you the confidence to trust God, even in the midst of uncertainty. One of the greatest challenges to devotion is distraction. In today's world, it's easy to get caught up in the busyness of life, to focus on things like social media, entertainment, or the pursuit of success. While none of these things are bad in themselves, they can easily take up so much of your time and attention that you have little left for God. Devotion requires intentionality. You have to make the choice to prioritize your relationship with God above all else. This might mean setting aside specific times each day for prayer and Bible study or finding ways to incorporate devotion into your daily routine. It's not always easy, but the rewards are worth it. When you devote yourself to God, you will find that He is faithful to meet you where you are. He will speak to you through His Word, give you strength through prayer, and guide you in ways you could never imagine. Another aspect of devotion is surrender. Devotion to God means that you are willing to lay down your own desires, plans, and ambitions in favor of His will. It means trusting that God's plans for your life are better than anything you could come up with on your own. This kind of surrender can be difficult, especially when you have dreams or goals that don't seem to line up with what God is calling you to do. But devotion means trusting that God knows what is best for you and that His ways are higher than your ways (Isaiah 55:8-9). When you are devoted to God, you are willing to let go of your own plans in order to follow His leading. Devotion also involves gratitude. When you devote yourself to God, you begin to see His hand at work in every area of your life. You start to recognize the ways He has blessed you, protected you, and provided for you. This awareness leads to a heart of gratitude, where you are continually thankful for God's goodness and faithfulness. Gratitude fuels your devotion, because the more you recognize what God has done for you, the more you want to live your life in a way that honors Him. In Colossians 3:17, Paul writes, "And whatsoever ye do in word or deed, do all in the name of the Lord Jesus, giving thanks to God and the Father by him." This verse highlights the importance of living a life of devotion that is marked by thankfulness. As you grow in your devotion to God, you will begin to see your life through the lens of His love and grace, and your response will be one of worship and gratitude. One of the most beautiful aspects of devotion is that it draws you closer to the heart of God. The more time you spend with Him in prayer and in His Word, the more you come to know Him in a personal and intimate way. Devotion is not just about following a set of rules or checking off spiritual tasks; it's about building a relationship with your Creator. It's about knowing Him as your Father, your Friend, and your Savior. Through devotion, you come to experience the depth of God's love for you, and that love transforms every part of your life. As you devote yourself to God, you will find that He is always with you, guiding you, comforting you, and leading you in the path of righteousness. Your devotion will lead you to a life of purpose, peace, and fulfillment, as you walk in the calling that God has placed on your life. Devotion is not something you do for a season; it's a lifelong journey. Every day, you have the opportunity to renew your commitment to God, to spend time in His presence, and to grow in your understanding of His Word. As you continue on this journey of devotion, you will find that your faith becomes stronger, your love for God grows deeper, and your life is filled with the joy and peace that come from knowing Him. So, as a young man seeking to build strong faith, make devotion to God a priority in your life. Let His Word be the foundation upon which you build your life, and let prayer be the constant connection that keeps you rooted in His love. Devote yourself to knowing God, to following His ways, and to living a life that reflects His glory. In doing so, you will not only strengthen your faith, but you will also experience the fullness of life that God has promised to those who love Him. With devotion as your guide, you can face the challenges of life with confidence, knowing that you are walking in the light of God's truth and living in the power of His love.

Chapter 4 - Diligence

Diligence is a key factor in building strong faith as a young man, as it involves working hard and staying committed both in your spiritual life and in your everyday responsibilities. To be diligent means that you don't just sit back and wait for things to happen; instead, you put in the effort, the time, and the focus necessary to grow and succeed in the areas that matter most. In both your walk with God and your responsibilities in the world—whether that be in school, at work, or in your relationships—diligence is what sets you apart as someone who is reliable, dedicated, and purposeful. Proverbs 10:4 says, "He becometh poor that dealeth with a slack hand: but the hand of the diligent maketh rich." This verse reminds us that laziness or a lack of effort leads to poverty, not just financially but also spiritually. If you neglect your responsibilities, whether in your faith or in your daily life, you will find yourself lacking. But when you work diligently, you will experience growth, success, and the rich rewards of your labor. Diligence in your spiritual life means putting in the effort to spend time with God, to study His Word, and to apply His teachings to your life. Just as an athlete trains every day to get stronger, your spiritual growth requires daily commitment and hard work. You can't expect to grow in your faith if you only pray once in a while or read your Bible occasionally. Diligence means being consistent, even when you're busy or when it feels difficult to stay focused. When you are diligent in your spiritual walk, you will begin to see how God moves in your life in powerful ways, guiding you, strengthening you, and helping you become the man He created you to be. Diligence also involves being persistent. There will be times when you don't see immediate results, whether in your spiritual growth or in other areas of your life. You may feel like you're working hard but not making progress. In these moments, it's important to remember that diligence is about continuing to put in the effort, even when the results aren't immediate. In 2 Peter 1:10, we are urged to "give diligence to make your calling and election sure." This means that we must actively pursue the things of God, confirming our commitment to Him through our actions, our choices, and our devotion. Being diligent in your faith is not just about avoiding sin or attending church; it's about wholeheartedly pursuing God, seeking to understand His will for your life, and making choices that honor Him. When you are diligent in your faith, you are showing God that you are serious about following Him and living according to His purpose. In your everyday responsibilities, diligence is equally important. Whether you're in school, working a job, or helping out at home, diligence means giving your best effort, staying focused, and following through on your commitments. When you are diligent in these areas, you are reflecting the character of Christ, who calls us to work "as unto the Lord" (Colossians 3:23). This means that no matter what task you are given, whether it's big or small, you should do it to the best of your ability, knowing that your hard work honors God. Diligence at school, for example, means studying hard, staying on top of your assignments, and striving for excellence, not because you're trying to impress others, but because you recognize that your efforts matter to God. Likewise, in your job or any other responsibility, being diligent means showing up on time, working hard, and being reliable. People will notice your diligence, and it will open doors for you, whether it's in building trust with others or in gaining new opportunities. Diligence is not about being perfect or never making mistakes, but it's about having the determination to keep going, to keep trying, and to keep growing. The Bible is full of examples of diligence, and one of the clearest is the story of Joseph. Despite facing incredible challenges—being sold into slavery by his brothers, falsely accused, and thrown into prison—Joseph remained diligent in his work and in his faith. He worked hard no matter where he was, and because of his diligence, God blessed him and elevated him to a position of great influence. Joseph's story reminds us that even in difficult circumstances, diligence can lead to success, and God can use our hard work for His glory. Another powerful example of diligence is found in the life of Nehemiah. When Nehemiah saw that the walls of Jerusalem were broken down, he was determined to do something about it. He didn't wait for someone else to take action; instead, he diligently led the effort to rebuild the walls, despite facing opposition and challenges along the way. Nehemiah's diligence and determination not only helped restore the city but also strengthened the faith of the people around him. His story shows us that when we are diligent in following God's call, we can accomplish great things, even in the face of obstacles. Diligence also involves being faithful in the small things. In Luke 16:10, Jesus says, "He that is faithful in that which is least is faithful also in much." This means that when you are diligent in the small, everyday tasks, God can trust you with greater responsibilities. Whether it's helping around the house, being kind to a friend, or staying focused in your studies, these small acts of diligence are important. They build character, discipline, and integrity, and they prepare you for the bigger opportunities God has for you in the future. Diligence is not always easy, especially in a world that often encourages shortcuts, quick fixes, and instant gratification. But as a young man of faith, you are called to a higher standard. You are called to be diligent in pursuing God's best for your life, even when it requires hard work, patience, and perseverance. This kind of diligence is not something you can achieve on your own; it requires relying on God's strength and wisdom. In Proverbs 3:5-6, we are reminded to "Trust in the LORD with all thine heart; and lean not unto thine own understanding. In all thy ways acknowledge him, and he shall direct thy paths." When you commit to being diligent, you can trust that God will guide your steps, provide for your needs, and help you succeed in His perfect timing. Diligence also involves setting goals and staying focused on what's important. In your spiritual life, this might mean setting a goal to read the Bible every day, to spend time in prayer, or to memorize Scripture. In your worldly responsibilities, it could mean setting goals for your education, your career, or your personal growth. Being diligent means staying focused on these goals, even when distractions come your way or when things get tough. It means being intentional about how you spend your time, making sure that your actions align with your priorities. Diligence requires discipline, but it also brings great rewards. When you are diligent in your spiritual walk, you will experience a deeper relationship with God, greater clarity about His purpose for your life, and a stronger sense of peace and joy. When you are diligent in your worldly responsibilities, you will see the fruits of your labor, whether it's in your academic success, your personal growth, or the trust and respect you earn from others. Diligence brings fulfillment because it allows you to live in alignment with God's will and to make the most of the opportunities He has given you. But perhaps the greatest reward of diligence is the knowledge that you are living a life that honors God. In 1 Corinthians 15:58, Paul writes, "Therefore, my beloved brethren, be ye stedfast, unmoveable, always abounding in the work of the Lord, forasmuch as ye know that your labour is not in vain in the Lord." When you are diligent in your work, whether it's in your faith or in your daily responsibilities, you can be confident that your efforts are not in vain.

God sees your hard work, and He is pleased when you serve Him with diligence and dedication. As you continue to build your faith and grow as a young man, remember that diligence is not something that comes naturally; it's something you develop over time. It requires effort, perseverance, and a willingness to trust God's plan for your life. But as you commit to being diligent, you will see how God blesses your efforts, strengthens your faith, and helps you succeed in ways you never thought possible. So be diligent in all that you do, knowing that your hard work will not only lead to success in this life but will also bring glory to God.

Chapter 5 - Discretion

Discretion is a vital quality for a young man seeking to build strong faith and live a life that honors God. It involves exercising wisdom and discernment in your choices, relationships, and how you navigate the challenges of life. Discretion means thinking carefully before acting, understanding the consequences of your decisions, and choosing what aligns with God's Word. It is about knowing when to speak and when to remain silent, who to trust and who to avoid, and when to take action or wait patiently for God's guidance. Proverbs 2:11 says, "Discretion shall preserve thee, understanding shall keep thee." This verse highlights the protective power of discretion. When you are thoughtful and discerning in your actions, you avoid many dangers and pitfalls that could harm your faith, reputation, or future. Discretion helps you steer clear of temptations and harmful influences that could lead you away from God's path. In a world full of distractions, temptations, and pressures, discretion is the shield that guards your heart and mind, keeping you focused on God's plan for your life. Proverbs 3:21-22 adds, "My son, let not them depart from thine eyes: keep sound wisdom and discretion: So shall they be life unto thy soul, and grace to thy neck." These verses remind us that discretion, paired with wisdom, brings life, peace, and grace. Wisdom and discretion go hand in hand because you need wisdom to discern what is right and wrong, good and bad, wise and foolish. Discretion gives you the ability to apply that wisdom to everyday situations and relationships, making choices that reflect God's truth and honor His will. As a young man, discretion is essential in your relationships. The people you surround yourself with have a significant influence on your life. Discretion helps you choose friends who encourage your faith, build you up, and share your values. It also helps you avoid those who may lead you into temptation, trouble, or bad decisions. Proverbs 13:20 says, "He that walketh with wise men shall be wise: but a companion of fools shall be destroyed." Discretion enables you to discern which relationships are healthy and which are harmful. When you use discretion in choosing your friends and companions, you are protecting your spiritual growth and making sure that your relationships bring you closer to God rather than pulling you away. Discretion also plays a crucial role in your speech. Proverbs 21:23 says,

"Whoso keepeth his mouth and his tongue keepeth his soul from troubles." Learning when to speak and when to be silent is a sign of maturity and spiritual wisdom. Discretion helps you avoid saying things you'll later regret or words that could hurt others. It guides you to speak with kindness, honesty, and respect, reflecting the character of Christ. When you practice discretion in your speech, you build stronger relationships, avoid unnecessary conflicts, and reflect the love and wisdom of God in your conversations. In your decision-making, discretion is equally important. Life is full of choices, and some decisions can have long-lasting consequences. Discretion helps you think through the potential outcomes before you act. Instead of rushing into decisions based on emotions, pressure, or what others are doing, discretion allows you to pause, pray, and seek God's guidance. James 1:5 says, "If any of you lack wisdom, let him ask of God, that giveth to all men liberally, and upbraideth not; and it shall be given him." When you ask God for wisdom and use discretion in your choices, you align yourself with His will and avoid many mistakes that could lead to regret or harm. Discretion also helps you set boundaries in your life. As a young man, you will face temptations and situations that challenge your values and faith. Discretion helps you recognize when something is not good for you, even if it seems appealing in the moment. It enables you to set clear boundaries in your relationships, your activities, and your personal life, keeping you on the path that God has for you. By exercising discretion, you protect your purity, your integrity, and your testimony as a follower of Christ. This quality also helps you avoid peer pressure, which can be especially strong during your teenage years and early adulthood. Discretion helps you stand firm in your convictions, even when others around you are making poor choices or pressuring you to conform to the world's standards. Romans 12:2 reminds us, "And be not conformed to this world: but be ye transformed by the renewing of your mind, that ye may prove what is that good, and acceptable, and perfect, will of God." Discretion enables you to resist the temptation to follow the crowd and instead make decisions based on God's truth. It empowers you to be a leader, not a follower, guiding others by your example of wisdom, integrity, and faith. Another important aspect of discretion is learning how to handle conflict. In life, disagreements and misunderstandings are inevitable, but discretion teaches you how to respond with grace and wisdom. Instead of reacting in anger, frustration, or defensiveness, discretion helps you approach conflict with a calm and thoughtful attitude. Proverbs 15:1 says, "A soft answer turneth away wrath: but grievous words stir up anger." Discretion guides you to choose your words carefully and seek peaceful resolutions, showing others the love and humility of Christ in your interactions. In your spiritual life, discretion is necessary for discerning God's voice and following His direction. There will be times when you have to make important decisions, and it can be challenging to know what God wants you to do. Discretion helps you filter out distractions, worldly advice, and your own desires, allowing you to focus on what God is saying. It involves seeking wise counsel from godly mentors, praying for discernment, and trusting God's timing. Isaiah 30:21 says, "And thine ears shall hear a word behind thee, saying, This is the way, walk ye in it, when ye turn to the right hand, and when ye turn to the left." Discretion enables you to listen for that still, small voice of God and follow His guidance, even when it requires patience or stepping out in faith. Discretion also keeps you humble. It reminds you that you don't have all the answers and that you need God's wisdom to make the right choices. Proverbs 11:2 says, "When pride cometh, then cometh shame: but with the lowly is wisdom." A discreet young man is one who recognizes his dependence on God and seeks His direction in all things. Discretion leads to humility because it acknowledges that we are not wise in our own eyes but that true wisdom comes from God. As you grow in your faith and maturity, discretion will help you avoid the pitfalls of pride and arrogance, leading you to live a life that honors God and blesses others. Discretion is also key in managing your time and priorities. As a young man, you have many demands on your time—school, work, friendships, family, hobbies, and more. Discretion helps you wisely manage your time by discerning what is most important and what aligns with your goals and values. Ephesians 5:15-16 says, "See then that ye walk circumspectly, not as fools, but as wise, redeeming the time, because the days are evil." Discretion enables you to make the most of your time by focusing on what matters most, avoiding distractions, and setting aside time for your spiritual growth and relationship with God. This includes making time for Bible study, prayer, fellowship with other believers, and serving others. By exercising discretion in how you spend your time, you will grow stronger in your faith and more effective in fulfilling God's purpose for your life. Discretion also protects you from making impulsive decisions that could lead to regret or harm. Proverbs 19:2 warns, "Also, that the soul be without knowledge, it is not good; and he that hasteth with his feet sinneth." When you rush into decisions without thinking them through or seeking God's wisdom, you are more likely to make mistakes that could hurt you or others. Discretion helps you slow down, consider the consequences, and choose the path that leads to life and blessing. It reminds you that some decisions are worth taking the time to pray about, seek counsel for, and reflect on before taking action. Discretion will also help you in your future career and professional life. As you enter the workforce, discretion will guide you in making ethical decisions, treating others with respect, and working with integrity. It will help you navigate workplace challenges and conflicts in a way that honors God and builds your reputation as a trustworthy and diligent worker. Proverbs 22:29 says, "Seest thou a man diligent in his business? He shall stand before kings; he shall not stand before mean men." When you exercise discretion in your work and your interactions with others, you open doors for opportunities, promotions, and success. Ultimately, discretion is a reflection of your relationship with God. It shows that you are committed to living according to His wisdom, that you value His guidance, and that you desire to make choices that please Him. As you grow in discretion, you will find that your life becomes more peaceful, purposeful, and aligned with God's will. Discretion preserves you from harm, helps you build strong relationships, and leads you to make decisions that honor God and bless others. It is a vital tool in your spiritual toolbox, equipping you to navigate the complexities of life with wisdom, grace, and discernment. So, as you seek to build strong faith as a young man, make discretion a priority. Let God's wisdom guide your choices, protect your heart, and lead you on the path of righteousness. Trust that as you exercise discretion in your relationships, decisions, and daily life, God will bless your efforts, strengthen your faith, and use you for His glory. In all that you do, keep sound wisdom and discretion close to your heart, and you will experience the life and grace that come from walking in God's ways.

Chapter 6 - Dependence

Dependence on God is a vital aspect of building strong faith as a young man. It means learning to rely on Him fully for your strength, wisdom, and provision, rather than trusting in your own abilities or understanding. In life, there will be many situations where you may feel overwhelmed, unsure of what to do, or lacking in resources. It is in these moments that dependence on God becomes essential. Proverbs 3:5-6 reminds us to "Trust in the LORD with all thine heart; and lean not unto thine own understanding. In all thy ways acknowledge him, and he shall direct thy paths." This verse teaches us that we cannot always rely on our own knowledge or reasoning because our perspective is limited, and we do not always see the bigger picture. However, God is all-knowing and all-powerful. He sees what we cannot see and knows what we do not know, and because of that, He calls us to trust Him completely. When you choose to depend on God, you are placing your life in His hands and acknowledging that He knows what is best for you, even when you don't understand what is happening around you. This trust is not just for the big moments in life but for every situation, whether small or large. As a young man, there may be many times when you feel the pressure to figure things out on your own, to prove your independence or strength. Society often teaches us to rely on ourselves and to take pride in our own accomplishments. While hard work and responsibility are important, the Bible teaches us that true strength comes from depending on God, not on ourselves. Philippians 4:19 assures us that "But my God shall supply all your need according to his riches in glory by Christ Jesus." This promise reminds us that God is our ultimate provider. Whether it's your physical needs, emotional support, or spiritual guidance, God has promised to provide for you according to His riches, which are far greater than anything you could ever attain on your own. When you depend on God, you are placing your faith in His ability to meet all of your needs. He is not limited by the challenges you face, the resources you have, or the obstacles in your way. He owns everything, controls everything, and has the power to do anything. Dependence on God also means relying on Him for wisdom. As you grow and face more decisions in life—whether about your education, career, relationships, or future—you will need God's guidance. Proverbs 3:5-6 tells us to "acknowledge him" in all our ways, and when we do, He will direct our paths. This means bringing every decision before God in prayer and asking for His wisdom before you act. James 1:5 says, "If any of you lack wisdom, let him ask of God, that giveth to all men liberally, and upbraideth not; and it shall be given him." God is generous in giving wisdom to those who seek it, and when you depend on Him for direction, He will guide you in the right way, protecting you from making wrong decisions based on limited or faulty information. Sometimes, the hardest part of dependence is surrendering your own plans and desires to God's will. You may have your own dreams, goals, and ideas of what you want your life to look like, but dependence on God requires you to trust that His plans are better. Jeremiah 29:11 tells us, "For I know the thoughts that I think toward you, saith the LORD, thoughts of peace, and not of evil, to give you an expected end." God's plans for you are always for your good, even when you cannot see how things will work out. Dependence on Him means that you trust His timing, His methods, and His outcomes, even when they don't align with your immediate desires. Sometimes, dependence on God also requires patience. There will be times when it feels like God is silent, or that He isn't answering your prayers in the way you expected. But depending on God means waiting on Him with faith, trusting that He is working behind the scenes, even when you can't see the results. Isaiah 40:31 promises, "But they that wait upon the LORD shall renew their strength; they shall mount up with wings as eagles; they shall run, and not be weary; and they shall walk, and not faint." When you wait on God, He renews your strength, giving you the energy and endurance you need to keep going, even when the journey is tough. Dependence on God also means trusting Him for strength in your weakest moments. As a young man, you may sometimes feel like you have to carry the weight of the world on your shoulders, whether it's dealing with personal struggles, responsibilities, or the expectations placed on you by others. But God invites you to bring your burdens to Him and to lean on His strength instead of your own. In Matthew 11:28-30, Jesus says, "Come unto me, all ye that labour and are heavy laden, and I will give you rest. Take my yoke upon you, and learn of me; for I am meek and lowly in heart: and ye shall find rest unto your souls. For my yoke is easy, and my burden is light." When you depend on God, you no longer have to carry your burdens alone. He offers you rest, peace, and relief, even in the most challenging times. Depending on God also changes the way you respond to fear and anxiety. Life is filled with uncertainties, and it's natural to feel afraid or anxious about the future. However, when you depend on God, you can rest in the assurance that He is in control. Philippians 4:6-7 encourages us, "Be careful for nothing; but in every thing by prayer and supplication with thanksgiving let your requests be made known unto God. And the peace of God, which passeth all understanding, shall keep your hearts and minds through Christ Jesus." Instead of being consumed by worry, dependence on God allows you to bring your concerns to Him in prayer, trusting that He will take care of you. This trust brings a peace that surpasses human understanding—a peace that guards your heart and mind, even in the midst of trials. Dependence on God is not a sign of weakness, but of true strength. It takes humility to admit that you cannot do everything on your own, and that you need God's help. 2 Corinthians 12:9 says, "And he said unto me, My grace is sufficient for thee: for my strength is made perfect in weakness. Most gladly therefore will I rather glory in my infirmities, that the power of Christ may rest upon me." God's grace is sufficient for every weakness you face. When you depend on Him, His power is revealed in your life in ways that far exceed what you could accomplish on your own. Dependence on God also involves relying on Him for provision. Whether it's financial needs, emotional support, or spiritual growth, God is your provider. Philippians 4:19 reminds us, "But my God shall supply all your need according to his riches in glory by Christ Jesus." No matter what you lack, God is able to provide because His resources are limitless. When you depend on God, you trust that He will meet every need you have, according to His perfect will. Sometimes, His provision comes in unexpected ways, but it is always exactly what you need at the right time. Dependence on God also brings freedom. When you stop trying to control everything and instead place your life in God's hands, you experience a sense of peace and freedom that comes from knowing that you don't have to figure everything out on your own. Matthew 6:33-34 encourages us, "But seek ye first the kingdom of God, and his righteousness; and all these things shall be added unto you. Take therefore no thought for the morrow: for the morrow shall take thought for the things of itself." When you prioritize your relationship with God and depend on Him, He takes care of the details. You no longer have to be weighed down by the worries of tomorrow because you know that God is already there, working everything out for your good. Dependence on

God also transforms your prayer life. When you depend on God, you recognize your need for constant communication with Him. Prayer becomes more than just asking for things; it becomes an ongoing conversation with the One who sustains you. 1 Thessalonians 5:17 encourages us to "Pray without ceasing." When you depend on God, you learn to bring every aspect of your life to Him in prayer—your fears, your joys, your struggles, and your decisions. Through prayer, you grow closer to God, deepening your trust in Him and experiencing His presence in your everyday life. Dependence on God also builds your faith. As you trust Him for strength, wisdom, and provision, you will begin to see how He answers your prayers and guides your steps. Each time you experience God's faithfulness, your faith grows stronger, making it easier to trust Him in the future. Psalm 37:5 encourages us, "Commit thy way unto the LORD; trust also in him; and he shall bring it to pass." Dependence on God is not just a one-time decision but a daily commitment to trust Him with every area of your life. As you do, you will see His hand at work in ways that strengthen your faith and deepen your relationship with Him. In conclusion, dependence on God is a foundational aspect of building strong faith as a young man. It means recognizing that you cannot do everything on your own and that you need God's strength, wisdom, and provision. It involves trusting Him in every situation, whether big or small, and allowing Him to guide your steps, provide for your needs, and strengthen you in your weakness. Dependence on God brings peace, freedom, and joy, knowing that He is in control and

that His plans for your life are good. As you grow in your dependence on God, you will experience the fullness of His love, grace, and power in your life, leading you to live with confidence and faith in the One who holds your future.

Chapter 7 - Direction

Seeking direction from God is one of the most important aspects of building strong faith as a young man. In life, you will face many decisions, big and small, that can shape your future and determine the kind of person you become. Whether it's choosing the right friends, deciding on a career path, or navigating the complexities of relationships, you need God's guidance in every step you take. Dependence on your own wisdom often leads to confusion, mistakes, and regret, but when you trust God to direct your path, you can be confident that He will lead you in the way that is best for you. Psalm 37:23 says, "The steps of a good man are ordered by the LORD: and he delighteth in his way." This verse reminds us that God is actively involved in our lives, guiding our steps and delighting in the path we take when we follow His will. Seeking God's direction means that you are acknowledging that His way is better than your own and that you trust Him to lead you toward His perfect plan for your life. One of the most beautiful aspects of following God's direction is the peace that comes with knowing He is in control. Life is full of uncertainties, and it's easy to feel overwhelmed by the pressure to make the right decisions. You may worry about whether you are on the right track or fear making a choice that could lead to failure or disappointment. But when you seek God's guidance, you can rest in the assurance that He knows the way forward. Proverbs 16:9 tells us, "A man's heart deviseth his way: but the LORD directeth his steps." This verse highlights the contrast between our human plans and God's divine direction. While it's natural for us to make plans and set goals, it's crucial to remember that the ultimate direction comes from God. He sees the bigger picture, knows what is best for you, and will lead you toward His purpose if you allow Him to guide your steps. Seeking God's direction starts with a humble heart. It requires you to recognize that you don't have all the answers and that you need God's wisdom to make the right choices. Proverbs 3:5-6 urges us to "Trust in the LORD with all thine heart; and lean not unto thine own understanding. In all thy ways acknowledge him, and he shall direct thy paths." This means surrendering your desire to control every aspect of your life and instead trusting God to lead you. It means seeking His guidance through prayer, reading His Word, and listening for His voice in every decision you make. When you approach God with humility and ask for His direction, He promises to guide you. One of the ways God provides direction is through His Word. The Bible is filled with wisdom, instruction, and principles that help us make decisions that honor God and reflect His will. Psalm 119:105 says, "Thy word is a lamp unto my feet, and a light unto my path." God's Word illuminates the way forward, helping you navigate through the challenges and uncertainties of life. When you study Scripture and apply its truths to your decisions, you are aligning your life with God's direction. His Word provides clarity when you are unsure, encouragement when you are discouraged, and guidance when you are lost. Another important aspect of seeking God's direction is prayer. Prayer is a direct line of communication between you and God, and it's through prayer that you can seek His will for your life. Philippians 4:6-7 reminds us, "Be careful for nothing; but in every thing by prayer and supplication with thanksgiving let your requests be made known unto God. And the peace of God, which passeth all understanding, shall keep your hearts and minds through Christ Jesus." When you bring your decisions before God in prayer, you are inviting Him to take control and lead you in the right direction. Prayer is not just about asking for things; it's about seeking God's presence, listening for His voice, and submitting your will to His. Through prayer, God can give you the wisdom, clarity, and peace you need to make the right decisions. One of the challenges of seeking God's direction is learning to trust His timing. Sometimes, we want answers right away, and we may feel frustrated or impatient when God doesn't reveal His plan immediately. But part of seeking God's direction is learning to wait on Him. Isaiah 40:31 encourages us, "But they that wait upon the LORD shall renew their strength; they shall mount up with wings as eagles; they shall run, and not be weary; and they shall walk, and not faint." Waiting on God's direction is not passive; it's an active trust that He is working behind the scenes, even when you can't see it. While you wait, God is preparing you, strengthening you, and aligning circumstances for His perfect will. Waiting on God teaches you patience, builds your faith, and deepens your relationship with Him. Another aspect of seeking God's direction is being open to His leading, even when it's different from what you expected. Sometimes, God's direction may take you down a path that is unfamiliar or uncomfortable, but trusting Him means being willing to follow where He leads, even when it doesn't make sense to you at the moment. Proverbs 14:12 warns, "There is a way which seemeth right unto a man, but the end thereof are the ways of death." Just because a path seems right in your eyes doesn't mean it's the best one. God's direction may not always align with your plans, but it's always for your good. Romans 8:28 reassures us, "And we know that all things work together for good to them that love God, to them who are the called according to his purpose." When you follow God's direction, you can trust that He is working everything out for your benefit, even if the road is difficult. Seeking God's direction also means being sensitive to the leading of the Holy Spirit. As a believer, the Holy Spirit lives within you, guiding you, convicting you, and helping you discern God's will. John 16:13 says, "Howbeit when he, the Spirit of truth, is come, he will guide you into all truth." The Holy Spirit is your guide, helping you navigate the complexities of life and revealing God's truth to you. When you cultivate a relationship with the Holy Spirit through prayer and obedience, you become more attuned to His voice, and He directs your steps. There may be times when you sense a nudge from the Holy Spirit, prompting you to take a certain action or avoid a particular situation. These promptings are part of God's direction, and it's important to listen and obey, even if you don't fully understand why at the moment. Obedience to God's direction is key to experiencing His blessings. Seeking direction is not just about hearing from God but also about following through on what He reveals. James 1:22 instructs us, "But be ye doers of the word, and not hearers only, deceiving your own selves." When God gives you direction, it's your responsibility to act on it. Obedience often requires faith, especially when God's direction leads you into unfamiliar territory or challenges you to step out of your comfort zone. But when you obey God, you open the door for His blessings and protection in your life. Sometimes, God's direction will involve taking risks or making sacrifices. It may mean letting go of something you value, trusting Him with your future, or making a difficult decision that others don't understand. But when you seek God's direction and obey His leading, you are living in alignment with His will, and that is the safest and most rewarding place to be. Another way God provides direction is through wise counsel. Proverbs 11:14 says, "Where no counsel is, the people fall: but in the multitude of counsellors there is safety." Surrounding yourself with godly mentors, pastors, or friends who share your faith can provide valuable guidance and insight. God often uses other people to speak into your life and confirm His direction for you. When you are faced with important decisions, seek the advice of those who have a strong relationship with God and who can offer biblical wisdom. At the same time, be careful to filter their advice through prayer and Scripture, ensuring that it aligns with what God is saying to you personally. It's also important to remember that seeking God's direction is a lifelong process. As you grow in your faith and mature in your relationship with God, you will continue to face new challenges and decisions that require His guidance. Proverbs 4:18 says, "But the path of the just is as the shining light, that shineth more and more unto the perfect day." Your journey with God is one of continual growth and discovery. As you seek His direction, He will reveal more of His purpose for your life and guide you step by step toward the destiny He has for you. There will be times when God's direction may not seem clear, and you may feel uncertain about which path to take. In these moments, trust that God is still with you, even if you don't have all the answers. Psalm 32:8 promises, "I will instruct thee and teach thee in the way which thou shalt go: I will guide thee with mine eye." God's guidance is constant, even when you can't see the full picture. Sometimes, He gives us just enough light for the next step, and we must trust Him to lead us as we go. When you are seeking direction, keep moving forward in faith, trusting that God will reveal the next step in His perfect timing. Ultimately, seeking God's direction is about developing a deep and abiding relationship with Him. It's about spending time in His presence, listening for His voice, and aligning your life with His will. As you grow in your relationship with God, seeking His direction will become second nature. You will learn to recognize His voice, trust

His leading, and follow His path with confidence. God desires to be involved in every aspect of your life, and when you invite Him to direct your steps, you will experience the fullness of His love, grace, and purpose. In conclusion, seeking God's direction is essential for building strong faith as a young man. It requires humility, trust, and a willingness to follow where God leads, even when the path is uncertain. Through prayer, Scripture, the Holy Spirit, and wise counsel, God provides the guidance you need to make decisions that honor Him and align with His will. As you seek His direction in every area of your life, you will experience His peace, protection, and provision, knowing that your steps are ordered by the Lord. Keep seeking, keep trusting, and keep following God's direction, and you will walk in the path He has prepared for you—a path that leads to life, blessing, and a deeper relationship with Him.

Chapter 8 - Defender of the Faith

Being a defender of the faith as a young man requires both determination and dedication to stand firm in your beliefs and uphold the truth of the Gospel, even in the face of opposition. The world today is filled with conflicting ideas, pressure to conform, and challenges to the truth of God's Word. As a young man seeking to build strong faith, you must be prepared to defend what you believe, not with aggression or hostility, but with confidence, grace, and unwavering conviction. 1 Peter 3:15 says, "But sanctify the Lord God in your hearts: and be ready always to give an answer to every man that asketh you a reason of the hope that is in you with meekness and fear." This verse highlights the importance of being prepared to explain your faith when people ask questions or challenge what you believe. It's not just about knowing what you believe, but also understanding why you believe it and being able to communicate that truth in a way that reflects the love and humility of Christ.

Defending the faith begins with sanctifying the Lord in your heart. This means making Christ the central focus of your life, allowing Him to shape your thoughts, actions, and words. When you set apart Christ as Lord, you are aligning your entire being with His truth, and this enables you to speak from a place of genuine faith. It's not about winning arguments or proving others wrong; it's about sharing the hope that you have in Christ and pointing others to the truth of the Gospel. Being a defender of the faith means you live in a way that reflects the reality of Christ in your life, so when people see you, they can see the difference that Jesus makes. This difference often opens the door for conversations about your faith, and that's when you need to be ready to give an answer.

Being ready to defend your faith requires preparation. This preparation comes from spending time in God's Word, learning the foundational truths of the Bible, and growing in your understanding of who God is and what He has done. Jude 1:3 tells us, "Ye should earnestly contend for the faith which was once delivered unto the saints." To contend for the faith means to stand up for the truth, to fight for what is right, and to protect the integrity of the Gospel. This does not mean physically fighting or being combative, but rather, it means being spiritually and mentally equipped to stand against false teachings, deception, and the pressures of the world that seek to undermine the truth of God's Word.

To earnestly contend for the faith, you must first know what the faith is. This means understanding the core doctrines of Christianity, such as the divinity of Jesus, His death and resurrection, salvation by grace through faith, and the authority of Scripture. When you know these truths deeply and personally, you will be able to recognize when they are being challenged or distorted. Studying the Bible and learning from mature Christians helps you grow in your knowledge and ability to defend the faith. It's important to not only know what the Bible says but also to understand how it applies to everyday life. When you can articulate the truth of the Gospel in a way that is relevant to the world around you, you become an effective defender of the faith.

Defending the faith also involves living it out. Your actions, character, and lifestyle should align with the truth of the Gospel. People are not only watching what you say but also how you live. When your life reflects the love, grace, and holiness of God, you are giving a powerful testimony to the truth of your faith. 1 Timothy 4:12 says, "Let no man despise thy youth; but be thou an example of the believers, in word, in conversation, in charity, in spirit, in faith, in purity." As a young man, you have the opportunity to be an example to others, showing them what it looks like to live a life committed to Christ. When you live with integrity and consistency, you give credibility to the message you are defending.

One of the most important aspects of defending the faith is doing so with love and humility. 1 Peter 3:15 encourages us to give an answer "with meekness and fear." This means we should approach conversations about faith with a spirit of gentleness and respect. It's easy to get defensive or argumentative when someone challenges your beliefs, but remember that the goal is not to win an argument, but to win a soul. Defending the faith is about leading people to the truth of Christ, and that is best done through love, patience, and understanding. Even when others are hostile or dismissive, you are called to respond in a way that honors God and reflects His character.

Another key part of being a defender of the faith is being able to recognize false teachings and deceptive philosophies that go against God's Word. In today's world, there are many ideas and beliefs that contradict the Bible, and it's important to be discerning. Colossians 2:8 warns, "Beware lest any man spoil you through philosophy and vain deceit, after the tradition of men, after the rudiments of the world, and not after Christ." As you grow in your faith, you must learn to compare what you hear and see with the truth of Scripture. When you know the Bible well, you will be able to discern what is true and what is false, and you can help others do the same.

In addition to studying the Bible and growing in knowledge, prayer is essential to defending the faith. Prayer is your direct connection to God, and through prayer, you can ask for wisdom, guidance, and strength to stand firm in your beliefs. James 1:5 encourages us, "If any of you lack wisdom, let him ask of God, that giveth to all men liberally, and upbraideth not; and it shall be given him." When you are faced with challenges to your faith, or when you are unsure how to respond to someone's questions or objections, turn to God in prayer. He will give you the wisdom and courage you need to defend the truth.

Defending the faith can sometimes feel intimidating, especially when you face opposition from the world. You may encounter people who mock your beliefs, question your faith, or try to convince you that you are wrong. In these moments, it's important to remember that you are not alone. God is with you, and He will strengthen you to stand firm. Ephesians 6:10-11 says, "Finally, my brethren, be strong in the Lord, and in the power of his might. Put on the whole armour of God, that ye may be able to stand against the wiles of the devil." The armor of God includes the belt of truth, the breastplate of righteousness, the shield of faith, the helmet of salvation, the sword of the Spirit (which is the Word of God), and the shoes of the gospel of peace. When you equip yourself with these spiritual tools, you are prepared to defend the faith against any attack.

Being a defender of the faith also means encouraging and strengthening other believers. Hebrews 10:24-25 reminds us, "And let us consider one another to provoke unto love and to good works: not forsaking the assembling of ourselves together, as the manner of some is; but exhorting one another: and so much the more, as ye see the day approaching." Standing firm in your faith is not something you have to do alone. You are part of a larger community of believers who can support and encourage you as you grow in your faith. By sharing your experiences, studying the Bible together, and praying for one another, you can help each other remain strong in the truth of the Gospel.

There will be times when defending the faith requires courage. It's not always easy to stand up for what you believe, especially when it goes against the flow of the culture around you. But God calls us to be bold in our witness for Him. 2 Timothy 1:7 says, "For God hath not given us the spirit of fear; but of power, and of love, and of a sound mind." When you feel afraid or unsure, remember that God has given you the power to stand firm. He will give you the words to say, the strength to endure, and the confidence to speak the truth in love.

Ultimately, being a defender of the faith is about glorifying God and pointing others to Jesus. Your goal is to share the hope of salvation with a world that desperately needs it. John 14:6 reminds us, "Jesus saith unto him, I am the way, the truth, and the life: no man cometh unto the Father, but by me." The message of the Gospel is the most important truth you can share, and defending that truth is an act of love toward those who are lost and searching for answers. When you defend the faith, you are participating in God's mission to bring people into a saving relationship with Him.

In conclusion, being a defender of the faith requires determination, dedication, and a deep commitment to stand firm in the truth of the Gospel. It means being prepared to give an answer for the hope that is in you, contending for the faith with love and humility, and living out your beliefs in a way that reflects the character of Christ. As you study God's Word, grow in knowledge, and seek His guidance through prayer, you will become a strong and effective defender of the faith. Remember that you are not alone—God is with you, equipping you with His power and wisdom to stand firm. Be bold, be courageous, and always stand ready to defend the truth of the Gospel, for it is the power of God unto salvation for all who believe.

Chapter 9 - Delight in the Lord

Delighting in the Lord is one of the most fulfilling and important aspects of building strong faith as a young man. It means finding your deepest joy and satisfaction in your relationship with God rather than in the temporary pleasures and distractions of the world. In today's culture, you're constantly being told that happiness and fulfillment come from success, popularity, material possessions, or entertainment. But the truth is, none of these things can provide lasting joy or true contentment. They may bring momentary pleasure, but eventually, they leave you feeling empty, always searching for more. In contrast, when you delight in the Lord, you are turning your focus away from the fleeting things of this world and setting your heart on the One who can truly satisfy your soul. Psalm 37:4 says, "Delight thyself also in the LORD; and he shall give thee the desires of thine heart." This verse is a powerful promise that when you find your joy and fulfillment in God, He will not only meet your needs but will also shape your desires to align with His perfect will for your life.

Delighting in the Lord starts with a deep, personal relationship with Him. It's about spending time in His presence, getting to know Him through prayer and reading His Word, and allowing His love to fill your heart. The more you seek after God, the more you will begin to experience His goodness, faithfulness, and peace. You will find that the things of this world, which once seemed so important, fade in comparison to the joy that comes from knowing God. When you delight in the Lord, your perspective on life changes. Instead of chasing after worldly achievements or possessions, you begin to desire the things of God—His righteousness, His purpose, and His will. This doesn't mean that you can't enjoy the good things that life has to offer, but it means that your ultimate joy and satisfaction come from your relationship with God, not from the things around you.

One of the key ways to delight in the Lord is through worship. Worship is more than just singing songs in church; it's about expressing your love and gratitude to God in everything you do. When you worship God, you are declaring that He is the most important part of your life, and you are acknowledging that all good things come from Him. Worship shifts your focus away from yourself and your circumstances and directs it toward God's greatness. It reminds you of His power, His love, and His faithfulness. In times of joy, worship is a way to celebrate God's blessings. In times of struggle, worship becomes a source of strength and encouragement, as you remember that God is in control and that He is working all things together for your good. Nehemiah 8:10 tells us, "For the joy of the LORD is your strength." When you find your joy in the Lord, you are strengthened in your faith, no matter what challenges you may face.

Delighting in the Lord also involves trusting Him with your life. When you delight in God, you are saying, "Lord, I trust You. I know that Your plans for me are good, and I will follow where You lead." This kind of trust is built over time as you experience God's faithfulness in your life. The more you see how God provides, protects, and guides you, the more you learn to delight in Him, knowing that He is always working for your good. Proverbs 3:5-6 encourages us to "Trust in the LORD with all thine heart; and lean not unto thine own understanding. In all thy ways acknowledge him, and he shall direct thy paths." When you trust God fully, you can let go of anxiety, worry, and fear because you know that He is in control. This trust brings a deep sense of peace and joy, even in the midst of uncertainty.

Another way to delight in the Lord is by meditating on His Word. The Bible is filled with the promises and truths of God, and when you spend time reading and reflecting on Scripture, you are reminded of His goodness and love. Psalm 119:103 says, "How sweet are thy words unto my taste! yea, sweeter than honey to my mouth!" God's Word is a source of joy and guidance in your life, and as you meditate on it, you begin to see the world through His perspective. His Word strengthens your faith, renews your mind, and helps you to grow in your relationship with Him. When you delight in God's Word, you are filling your heart with His truth, which equips you to stand firm in your faith and resist the temptations of the world.

Delighting in the Lord is also about living a life of gratitude. When you delight in God, you recognize that every good thing in your life comes from Him, and you respond with thankfulness. 1 Thessalonians 5:18 says, "In every thing give thanks: for this is the will of God in Christ Jesus concerning you." Gratitude is a powerful way to shift your focus from what you lack to the abundance of God's blessings in your life. It helps you to appreciate the small, everyday gifts that God provides, and it reminds you of His faithfulness in both the big and small moments of life. When you cultivate a heart of gratitude, you are less likely to be swayed by the dissatisfaction and discontentment that the world often promotes. Instead, you are filled with the joy of knowing that God is taking care of you and that He is always good.

One of the greatest blessings of delighting in the Lord is the joy and peace that comes from being in His presence. Psalm 16:11 says, "Thou wilt shew me the path of life: in thy presence is fulness of joy; at thy right hand there are pleasures for evermore." When you make time to be in God's presence, whether through prayer, worship, or quiet reflection, you are filled with a sense of joy that the world cannot offer. This joy is not based on circumstances or material possessions, but on the unchanging love and goodness of God. It is a joy that sustains you through trials and difficulties, and it gives you strength to keep moving forward in faith.

Delighting in the Lord also involves serving others. When you experience the joy of the Lord in your life, you are motivated to share that joy with others. Serving others is a way to express your love for God and to reflect His character in the world. Galatians 5:13 says, "By love serve one another." When you serve others, whether through acts of kindness, encouragement, or meeting their needs, you are showing the love of Christ to those around you. This kind of selfless service brings joy to both you and those you serve, and it deepens your relationship with God as you live out His command to love your neighbor.

Another important aspect of delighting in the Lord is finding contentment in Him. The world constantly tells you that you need more—more money, more success, more possessions—in order to be happy. But true contentment comes from knowing that God is enough. Philippians 4:11-13 says, "Not that I speak in respect of want: for I have learned, in whatsoever state I am, therewith to be content. I know both how to be abased, and I know how to abound: every where and in all things I am instructed both to be full and to be hungry, both to abound and to suffer need. I can do all things through Christ which strengtheneth me." Contentment is not about having everything you want, but about trusting that God has given you everything you need. When you find your satisfaction in the Lord, you are freed from the constant pursuit of worldly things, and you are able to rest in the peace of knowing that God is your provider and sustainer.

Delighting in the Lord also means seeking His will for your life. As you grow in your relationship with God, your desires begin to align with His desires. Psalm 37:4 promises that when you delight in the Lord, "he shall give thee the desires of thine heart." This doesn't mean that God will give you everything you want, but rather that He will shape your desires to match His perfect will. When you delight in God, you begin to desire the things that honor Him and reflect His heart—things like love, justice, mercy, and righteousness. Your goals and dreams become centered on fulfilling His purpose for your life, and you find joy in pursuing the things that bring Him glory.

Delighting in the Lord is a lifelong journey. It's not something that happens overnight, but something that grows as you continue to seek God and experience His love. As you spend time in His presence, trust in His goodness, and align your life with His will, you will find that the joy and satisfaction that comes from knowing God far surpasses anything the world can offer. This joy is not dependent on circumstances, but on the unchanging character of God. It is a joy that sustains you through trials, gives you strength in weakness, and fills your heart with peace and contentment.

In conclusion, delighting in the Lord is about finding your deepest joy and satisfaction in your relationship with God rather than in the temporary things of the world. It involves worship, trust, gratitude, contentment, and service, all of which help you grow closer to God and experience the fullness of His love. As you delight in the Lord, you are filled with His joy, which becomes your strength, and you are able to live a life that reflects His goodness and brings glory to His name. When you make God the center of your life, you will discover that He truly is the source of all joy, peace, and fulfillment. So, delight yourself in the Lord, and let Him fill your heart with the desires that align with His perfect will for your life.

Chapter 10 - Determination

Determination is one of the most crucial qualities needed for building strong faith as a young man. It is the unwavering commitment to follow God's calling for your life, even when faced with trials, challenges, and obstacles. In a world filled with distractions, temptations, and opposition, staying determined in your walk with God is essential to growing spiritually and living out your purpose. Determination means not giving up, even when the path ahead seems difficult, and trusting that God will give you the strength and endurance to keep going. Galatians 6:9 encourages us, "And let us not be weary in well doing: for in due season we shall reap, if we faint not." This verse is a reminder that determination pays off. There may be times when it feels like your efforts to live a life pleasing to God are not yielding immediate results, but the Bible promises that if you don't give up, you will eventually reap the rewards of your faithfulness. God sees your efforts, your struggles, and your perseverance, and He promises that there will be a harvest of blessings if you remain determined.

Determination in your faith is about making a decision to follow God no matter what, and then sticking with that decision every day. It means waking up each morning with a renewed commitment to live for Christ, regardless of the challenges you may face. As a young man, there are many pressures that can try to pull you away from your faith—peer pressure, worldly temptations, doubts, and even personal struggles. But determination means standing firm in your faith, even when the world around you is pushing you in the opposite direction. This kind of determination doesn't come from your own strength; it comes from relying on God and trusting in His power to sustain you. James 1:12 says, "Blessed is the man that endureth temptation: for when he is tried, he shall receive the crown of life, which the Lord hath promised to them that love him." This verse reminds us that determination is not just about getting through easy times; it's about enduring temptation, trials, and difficulties, knowing that there is a greater reward waiting for those who remain steadfast.

One of the key aspects of determination is having a clear sense of purpose. When you know what God has called you to do, it gives you the focus and motivation you need to keep moving forward, even when things get tough. Proverbs 16:3 says, "Commit thy works unto the LORD, and thy thoughts shall be established." When you commit your life, your plans, and your goals to God, He will establish your path and give you the direction you need. Having a clear sense of God's calling helps you stay determined because it gives you something to hold onto when challenges arise. Instead of being swayed by circumstances or discouraged by setbacks, you can keep your eyes fixed on the purpose God has given you, knowing that He will guide you through every difficulty.

Determination also involves a willingness to persevere through trials. Life is full of ups and downs, and as a follower of Christ, you are not immune to hardships. In fact, the Bible tells us that we will face trials and difficulties as we seek to live for God. But determination means choosing to keep going, even when the road is hard. Romans 5:3-4 reminds us, "And not only so, but we glory in tribulations also: knowing that tribulation worketh patience; And patience, experience; and experience, hope." Trials are not meant to defeat you; they are meant to strengthen your faith and build your character. When you stay determined in the face of trials, you are allowing God to work in your life, shaping you into the person He wants you to be. Each trial you endure with determination brings you closer to God and helps you grow in maturity, faith, and trust in Him.

Another important aspect of determination is staying focused on what really matters. The world is full of distractions—things that seem important but ultimately pull you away from your relationship with God. Whether it's the pursuit of success, material possessions, or the desire to fit in with others, these distractions can easily take your focus off of God's calling for your life. But determination means keeping your priorities in order and staying focused on what truly matters—your relationship with God, your spiritual growth, and the mission He has given you. Colossians 3:2 reminds us, "Set your affection on things above, not on things on the earth." When you stay determined to keep your focus on God and His purposes, you will find that the distractions of the world lose their appeal. Instead of being consumed by temporary things, you will be filled with a deeper sense of purpose and fulfillment that comes from living for God.

Determination also means being willing to make sacrifices. Following God's calling often requires giving up things that may seem good or comfortable in the moment, but that ultimately hinder your spiritual growth. Whether it's letting go of unhealthy relationships, turning away from sinful habits, or making choices that set you apart from the world, determination involves being willing to sacrifice temporary pleasures for the sake of something greater—your relationship with God and the eternal rewards He promises. Matthew 16:24 says, "Then said Jesus unto his disciples, If any man will come after me, let him deny himself, and take up his cross, and follow me." Determination is about denying yourself and choosing to follow Christ, even when it's difficult or uncomfortable. It's about being willing to say no to things that may bring momentary satisfaction but ultimately lead you away from God's best for your life.

In addition to staying focused and making sacrifices, determination also involves relying on God's strength rather than your own. As a young man, it's easy to feel like you have to handle everything on your own—to be strong, independent, and self-sufficient. But the truth is, none of us can truly live for God in our own strength. We need His power and His guidance to stay determined in our faith. Philippians 4:13 reminds us, "I can do all things through Christ which strengtheneth me." Determination means acknowledging your need for God's help and relying on Him to give you the strength, wisdom, and courage you need to keep going. When you depend on God, you will find that He is always faithful to provide what you need, even when you feel weak or overwhelmed.

Determination is also about having a long-term perspective. It's easy to get discouraged when things don't happen as quickly as you want them to, or when you face setbacks along the way. But determination means looking beyond the immediate challenges and trusting that God is working in the bigger picture. Hebrews 12:1-2 encourages us, "Let us run with patience the race that is set before us, Looking unto Jesus the author and finisher of our faith." The Christian life is not a sprint; it's a marathon. It requires patience, perseverance, and a steadfast focus on Jesus, who has already gone before us and who will complete the good work He has started in us. When you keep your eyes on Jesus, you can stay determined, knowing that He is leading you toward the finish line and that the rewards of faithfulness far outweigh the temporary struggles you may face.

Another key aspect of determination is community. God never intended for us to walk the journey of faith alone. He has given us the gift of community—the church, friends, mentors, and other believers who can encourage us, support us, and help us stay determined in our faith. Ecclesiastes 4:9-10 says, "Two are better than one; because they have a good reward for their labour. For if they fall, the one will lift up his fellow." Surrounding yourself with people who share your commitment to Christ can help you stay determined, especially when you face challenges or feel discouraged. When you have others praying for you, encouraging you, and holding you accountable, it strengthens your resolve to keep following God's calling.

Determination also involves daily discipline. Building strong faith is not something that happens overnight; it's a process that requires consistent effort and intentional choices. It means setting aside time each day to spend with God in prayer, reading His Word, and seeking His guidance. Psalm 119:105 says, "Thy word is a lamp unto my feet, and a light unto my path." When you make it a priority to spend time in God's Word, it keeps you grounded in His truth and helps you stay focused on His calling. Daily discipline also involves making wise choices in how you spend your time, who you surround yourself with, and what you allow into your heart and mind. By being intentional in these areas, you are building a strong foundation that will help you stay determined, even when life gets difficult.

Finally, determination is about trusting in God's faithfulness. One of the greatest sources of strength in staying determined is knowing that God is faithful and that He will never leave you or forsake you. Deuteronomy 31:6 says, "Be strong and of a good courage, fear not, nor be afraid of them: for the LORD thy God, he it is that doth go with thee; he will not fail thee, nor forsake thee." When you face challenges or feel like giving up, remember that God is with you every step of the way. He has promised to be your strength, your guide, and your protector. You don't have to rely on your own abilities or figure everything out on your own. God is faithful, and He will carry you through every trial and difficulty.

In conclusion, determination is a vital part of building strong faith as a young man. It means staying steadfast in your commitment to follow God's calling, even when the road is hard. It involves having a clear sense of purpose, persevering through trials, staying focused on what really matters, making sacrifices, relying on God's strength, and trusting in His faithfulness. Determination is not about being perfect or never making mistakes, but it's about choosing to keep going, even when it's difficult, and trusting that God will reward your faithfulness in His perfect timing. As you stay determined in your walk with God, you will grow stronger in your faith, experience His presence in deeper ways, and ultimately fulfill the purpose He has for your life. So, stay determined, and keep running the race with endurance, knowing that God is with you every step of the way and that the rewards of faithfulness are far greater than anything this world can offer.

Chapter 11 - Discernment

Discernment is one of the most critical qualities a young man can develop as he builds strong faith, and it is essential for making wise decisions, navigating life's challenges, and staying on the path that God has set for you. Discernment is the ability to develop spiritual insight to distinguish between right and wrong, good and evil, truth and deception. In a world filled with conflicting messages, temptations, and influences that seek to pull you away from your faith, having the discernment to recognize what aligns with God's will and what does not is essential. Hebrews 5:14 tells us, "But strong meat belongeth to them that are of full age, even those who by reason of use have their senses exercised to discern both good and evil." This verse speaks to the spiritual maturity that comes through practice and experience in applying God's Word to your life. Discernment is not something that comes naturally; it is something that grows as you develop a deeper relationship with God, study His Word, and apply His truth in your daily life. It is through regular exercise—through prayer, meditation on Scripture, and seeking God's wisdom—that your spiritual senses become sharpened, allowing you to make decisions that honor God and lead you in the right direction.

The world around you is constantly trying to blur the lines between right and wrong, convincing you that what is harmful is actually good or that what pleases God is outdated or irrelevant. But as a young man seeking to build strong faith, it is crucial to resist these deceptions and remain grounded in God's truth. Proverbs 14:8 says, "The wisdom of the prudent is to understand his way: but the folly of fools is deceit." This verse reminds us that discernment helps us understand our way and keeps us from falling into the traps of foolishness and deception. The prudent young man is one who seeks God's wisdom before making decisions and who does not rush into things without carefully considering the consequences. He does not rely on his own understanding or follow the crowd but instead seeks to align his life with the truth of God's Word.

Discernment begins with a heart that is fully committed to seeking God's will above all else. Proverbs 3:5-6 instructs us, "Trust in the LORD with all thine heart; and lean not unto thine own understanding. In all thy ways acknowledge him, and he shall direct thy paths." When you trust in God and acknowledge Him in all your ways, you open yourself up to His guidance and direction. This means surrendering your own desires, opinions, and plans and asking God to show you His way. As you seek God's direction through prayer and the study of His Word, you will begin to see more clearly the distinction between what is right and what is wrong. God's Spirit within you will guide you into truth, helping you avoid the pitfalls of sin, temptation, and worldly influence.

One of the key elements of discernment is understanding that not everything that appears good is truly good. The enemy is often subtle, presenting temptations and false teachings that seem harmless or even beneficial at first glance. 2 Corinthians 11:14 warns, "And no marvel; for Satan himself is transformed into an angel of light." The enemy is skilled at disguising lies as truth, and without discernment, it's easy to be led astray by things that appear to be good on the surface but are actually harmful to your spiritual growth. This is why it is so important to develop discernment, so that you can see through the deceptions of the enemy and stand firm in the truth of God's Word.

Discernment also involves being able to separate your emotions and desires from God's will. Sometimes, what we want is not necessarily what is best for us, and our emotions can cloud our judgment. For example, you may desire something that feels good or seems right in the moment, but deep down, you know it doesn't align with God's plan for your life. Discernment helps you recognize when your emotions are leading you in the wrong direction and empowers you to make decisions based on God's truth rather than on temporary feelings. James 1:5 encourages us, "If any of you lack wisdom, let him ask of God, that giveth to all men liberally, and upbraideth not; and it shall be given him." When you seek God's wisdom, He will give you the discernment you need to make decisions that are in line with His will.

Another aspect of discernment is being able to identify and avoid false teachings. In today's world, there are many voices claiming to speak for God, but not all of them are rooted in the truth of Scripture. 1 John 4:1 warns, "Beloved, believe not every spirit, but try the spirits whether they are of God: because many false prophets are gone out into the world." Discernment allows you to test what you hear against the Word of God and to reject anything that does not align with biblical truth. It also helps you to recognize when teachings or influences are leading you away from God rather than toward Him. Whether it's through entertainment, media, or even well-meaning friends, discernment gives you the ability to filter what you are exposed to and make choices that keep you on the path of righteousness.

As a young man, it's important to recognize that discernment is not just about avoiding sin; it's also about pursuing what is good, true, and beneficial for your spiritual growth. Philippians 4:8 urges us, "Finally, brethren, whatsoever things are true, whatsoever things are honest, whatsoever things are just, whatsoever things are pure, whatsoever things are lovely, whatsoever things are of good report; if there be any virtue, and if there be any praise, think on these things." Discernment helps you focus your thoughts and actions on what is pleasing to God, rather than getting distracted by the things of the world. It empowers you to choose friendships, activities, and habits that build you up spiritually and bring you closer to God.

Discernment also plays a vital role in your relationships with others. As you grow in your faith, you will need discernment to navigate the complexities of friendships, dating relationships, and other interactions. Not everyone who enters your life is meant to stay, and not every relationship is healthy or beneficial for your spiritual walk. Discernment helps you recognize when a relationship is helping you grow closer to God and when it's pulling you away from Him. It also helps you determine how to handle conflicts, forgive others, and make wise decisions about who you surround yourself with. Proverbs 13:20 says, "He that walketh with wise men shall be wise: but a companion of fools shall be destroyed." Discernment enables you to choose companions who will encourage your faith, challenge you to grow, and support you in your walk with God.

Discernment is not just about making the right decisions for yourself; it's also about helping others. As you develop spiritual insight, you will be able to offer guidance and encouragement to those around you who may be struggling to see the truth. Galatians 6:1 reminds us, "Brethren, if a man be overtaken in a fault, ye which are spiritual, restore such an one in the spirit of meekness; considering thyself, lest thou also be tempted." Discernment allows you to speak truth into the lives of others with humility and love, helping them avoid the traps of sin and grow in their own faith. By offering wise counsel and support, you become a blessing to those around you and help build up the body of Christ.

To develop discernment, it's important to cultivate a close relationship with the Holy Spirit. The Holy Spirit is your guide, your teacher, and the One who leads you into all truth. John 16:13 says, "Howbeit when he, the Spirit of truth, is come, he will guide you into all truth." As you spend time in prayer and listen for the leading of the Holy Spirit, He will give you the discernment you need to navigate life's challenges and make decisions that honor God. The Holy Spirit also helps you recognize when something is not right, whether it's a temptation, a deceptive influence, or a wrong decision. By tuning your heart to the voice of the Holy Spirit, you will be able to discern God's will more clearly and avoid the snares of the enemy.

Developing discernment also requires patience and perseverance. It's not something that happens overnight, but something that grows as you continue to seek God and apply His Word to your life. Just as physical muscles are strengthened through regular exercise, your spiritual discernment is strengthened through consistent practice. Hebrews 5:14 tells us that discernment belongs to those who have "their senses exercised to discern both good and evil." This means that the more you use discernment in your daily life, the sharper it becomes. Each time you make a decision based on God's truth rather than on worldly influences or emotions, you are strengthening your ability to discern. Over time, you will become more attuned to God's guidance and more skilled at recognizing what is good and what is evil.

Another important aspect of discernment is humility. Recognizing that you don't have all the answers and that you need God's wisdom is a key part of developing discernment. Proverbs 11:2 says, "When pride cometh, then cometh shame: but with the lowly is wisdom." Humility allows you to be teachable and open to correction, which is essential for growing in discernment. When you are humble, you are willing to seek counsel from others, learn from your mistakes, and rely on God's wisdom rather than your own understanding. Humility also helps you avoid the trap of pride, which can lead to poor decisions and spiritual downfall. By cultivating a spirit of humility, you open yourself up to God's guidance and allow Him to lead you in the right direction.

In conclusion, discernment is a vital quality for building strong faith as a young man. It is the spiritual insight that allows you to distinguish between right and wrong, good and evil, truth and deception. Discernment helps you navigate the challenges of life, make wise decisions, and stay on the path that God has set for you. It begins with a heart that is fully committed to seeking God's will and is developed through prayer, study of God's Word, and reliance on the Holy Spirit. Discernment empowers you to avoid the traps of the enemy, pursue what is good, and make choices that align with God's truth. It also plays a key role in your relationships, helping you choose companions who will encourage your faith and allowing you to offer wise counsel to others. As you grow in discernment, you will become more attuned to God's guidance and more skilled at recognizing His will in your life. By practicing discernment, you will be able to navigate life's challenges with wisdom, stay faithful to God's calling, and experience the fullness of His blessings in your life.

Chapter 12 - Dependability

Dependability is a crucial characteristic for a young man seeking to build strong faith, as it involves being trustworthy, reliable, and faithful in your relationships with both God and others. It means consistently doing what you say you will do, following through on your commitments, and being someone that people can count on in every aspect of life. In a world where reliability is often overlooked and promises are easily broken, being a dependable person stands out as a reflection of God's faithfulness. Luke 16:10 teaches us, "He that is faithful in that which is least is faithful also in much." This verse reminds us that dependability begins with small actions. If you are reliable in the little things, God will trust you with bigger responsibilities. Dependability is about integrity, making sure that your actions match your words, and that people know they can count on you whether in big tasks or small, unnoticed moments. The value of being dependable cannot be overstated, especially when it comes to your relationship with God and your interactions with others.

To be dependable is to be faithful, and faithfulness is at the core of God's character. Throughout Scripture, God is described as faithful and unchanging, always keeping His promises and being there for His people. As a young man who wants to grow in faith, you are called to reflect this same quality in your own life. 1 Corinthians 4:2 says, "Moreover it is required in stewards, that a man be found faithful." Being a steward means being entrusted with something valuable, and for a believer, this often includes not only material possessions but also relationships, time, talents, and the calling God has placed on your life. Dependability means that you can be trusted to manage these gifts and responsibilities well, always striving to honor God in everything you do. Whether it's completing an assignment, showing up on time, or being there for a friend in need, dependability is about proving that you can be counted on, day in and day out.

In your relationship with God, dependability manifests as faithfulness to His Word, prayer, and obedience to His calling. It's about committing to your spiritual growth and consistently seeking to deepen your relationship with God, even when it's not easy or convenient. Just as God is always faithful to you, being dependable in your relationship with Him means that you prioritize your time with Him, you are consistent in prayer and Bible study, and you actively work to live out His commandments in your daily life. Dependability in your faith means that God can trust you to represent Him well in the world, sharing the Gospel, showing love to others, and living according to His principles. Proverbs 3:3 encourages us, "Let not mercy and truth forsake thee: bind them about thy neck; write them upon the table of thine heart." Dependability is about living in a way that consistently reflects God's truth and love, not just when it's convenient but in every situation.

One of the greatest ways to demonstrate dependability in your faith is by being obedient to God's commands, even when no one is watching. Dependability isn't about seeking recognition or applause for doing what's right—it's about doing the right thing simply because it honors God. In Matthew 6:1-4, Jesus warns against doing good deeds just for the praise of others, teaching that true righteousness comes from a heart that seeks to please God, not people. This is the essence of dependability in your walk with God: it's about being faithful and consistent in your actions, whether they are seen or unseen. God sees your heart, and when you are faithful in the small, private moments of your life, He knows He can trust you with greater responsibilities.

Dependability is also vital in your relationships with others. People need to know that they can trust you, that your word is reliable, and that you will be there for them when you say you will. This is especially important in friendships, family relationships, and in the workplace or school environment. Dependability builds trust, and trust is the foundation of any strong relationship. Proverbs 17:17 says, "A friend loveth at all times, and a brother is born for adversity." Being dependable means that you are someone who sticks by your friends and loved ones, especially in difficult times. When others are going through hardships or need support, they should be able to rely on you to offer a helping hand, a listening ear, or a word of encouragement. Dependability means showing up when it matters, and sometimes, it's in the smallest acts of kindness and consistency that you make the biggest impact on someone's life.

Dependability is also important when it comes to responsibilities. Whether you have a job, attend school, or have responsibilities at home, being dependable means taking those duties seriously and following through on your commitments. Colossians 3:23 says, "And whatsoever ye do, do it heartily, as to the Lord, and not unto men." This verse reminds us that dependability in our work or studies is a reflection of our commitment to God. When you approach your responsibilities with excellence, diligence, and faithfulness, you are honoring God and setting an example for others. Even in tasks that may seem mundane or unimportant, dependability matters because it shows that you are trustworthy and committed to doing your best in every situation. God sees your faithfulness in the small things and will bless you with greater opportunities as you prove yourself dependable.

Another aspect of dependability is consistency in your character. Being dependable means that people know they can trust you to act with integrity, no matter the circumstances. It means that you are the same person in private as you are in public, and that your values and actions align with your faith at all times. This kind of consistency is rare in today's world, where many people change their behavior based on who they're around or what they want to achieve. But as a young man of faith, you are called to be dependable in your character, living with integrity whether anyone is watching or not. Psalm 15:4 describes the kind of person who is dependable: "He that sweareth to his own hurt, and changeth not." This means that even when it's hard or inconvenient, you stick to your word and live out your commitments, because your integrity matters more than temporary comfort or approval.

Dependability also involves perseverance. There will be times in life when things get tough, when it feels easier to give up than to keep going. But being dependable means staying the course, even when it's difficult. Galatians 6:9 encourages us, "And let us not be weary in well doing: for in due season we shall reap, if we faint not." Dependability requires endurance—whether it's in your spiritual walk, your relationships, or your responsibilities, you need to be someone who keeps showing up, even when the path is hard or the results aren't immediate. Perseverance in dependability is a reflection of God's own faithfulness to us. He never gives up on us, even when we fall short or face difficulties. In the same way, you are called to be dependable, sticking with what's right and following through on your commitments, trusting that God will reward your faithfulness in His perfect timing.

Furthermore, dependability in your faith helps you build a strong testimony. When people see that you are reliable, consistent, and faithful in your relationship with God, it speaks volumes about the depth of your faith.

Dependability is a witness to others that your faith is not just words but is lived out in your daily actions. Matthew 5:16 reminds us, "Let your light so shine before men, that they may see your good works, and glorify your Father which is in heaven." Being dependable allows your light to shine brightly in a world that often values convenience over commitment. When you are dependable, people take notice, and your faith becomes a powerful testimony to God's work in your life.

Dependability also brings a sense of peace and security to those around you. In a world where so many things are uncertain and unreliable, being a dependable person gives others confidence and assurance that they can trust you. This kind of trustworthiness reflects the heart of God, who is described as our Rock, our refuge, and our ever-present help in times of trouble. When others know they can depend on you, it builds stronger relationships, deepens mutual respect, and allows for greater collaboration and support in both personal and community settings. Dependability fosters a sense of unity, as people work together, knowing that each person is committed to doing their part.

Additionally, dependability is a reflection of spiritual maturity. As you grow in your relationship with God, you should become more and more like Christ, who was the ultimate example of dependability. Jesus was faithful in every aspect of His life—faithful to His Father, faithful to His mission, and faithful to the people He served. Even when faced with immense challenges, temptations, and suffering, Jesus remained steadfast and dependable, fulfilling His calling all the way to the cross. Philippians 2:8 says, "And being found in fashion as a man, he humbled himself, and became obedient unto death, even the death of the cross." As a young man of faith, you are called to follow in Jesus' footsteps, becoming more dependable and faithful as you grow in your walk with God.

Dependability also requires humility. Being dependable isn't about seeking recognition or trying to impress others. It's about serving others selflessly and doing what is right because it honors God. Proverbs 27:2 advises, "Let another man praise thee, and not thine own mouth; a stranger, and not thine own lips." When you are dependable, you don't need to boast about your actions or seek praise from others. Your faithfulness and reliability will speak for themselves, and in time, others will come to respect and appreciate your dependability.

Humility in dependability also means being willing to admit when you've made a mistake or

fallen short and then working to make it right. Dependable people take responsibility for their actions and are committed to doing better, rather than making excuses or shifting blame.

Finally, dependability in your faith is a way of honoring God and reflecting His character to the world. God is always faithful, always reliable, and always true to His Word. When you strive to be dependable, you are reflecting God's own nature and bringing glory to Him. Psalm 89:8 says, "O LORD God of hosts, who is a strong LORD like unto thee? or to thy faithfulness round about thee?" Just as God is faithful to us, we are called to be faithful and dependable in all areas of our lives. When you live a life of dependability, you are demonstrating the faithfulness of God to a watching world, showing that His truth and His love are worth committing to, no matter the cost.

In conclusion, dependability is an essential part of building strong faith as a young man. It involves being trustworthy and reliable in your relationships with God and others, following through on your commitments, and living with integrity. Dependability reflects God's own faithfulness and is a testimony to the depth of your faith. Whether in small tasks or significant responsibilities, dependability matters because it builds trust, strengthens relationships, and honors God. As you grow in your faith, strive to be a dependable person, one who can be counted on in every situation, knowing that your faithfulness will not only bless those around you but will also bring glory to God. Dependability is a key part of living out your calling as a follower of Christ, and as you remain steadfast in your commitments, you will experience the joy, peace, and fulfillment that come from living a life that truly reflects God's character.

Conclusion

In conclusion, building strong faith as a young man requires determination and dedication to follow God in every aspect of your life. It's not always easy, but it's a journey worth every effort. The world will try to pull you in different directions, offering distractions, temptations, and challenges that make it hard to stay on the right path. But with determination, you can stand firm in your faith, trusting God to guide you through every trial. Dedication means making a commitment to grow in your relationship with Him—through prayer, reading His Word, and living out your faith daily. As you develop these qualities, you will experience God's strength and guidance, even when life gets tough. The Bible reminds us in Galatians 6:9, "And let us not be weary in well doing: for in due season we shall reap, if we faint not." Keep pressing forward, knowing that your dedication will bring you closer to God and that your efforts will not be in vain.

As you move forward in your walk with Christ, remember that your faith is a lifelong journey. You won't always have all the answers, and there will be times when you feel weak or uncertain. But that's where determination comes in—choosing to stay committed, even when it's hard. You can't rely on your own strength; instead, depend on God for the wisdom and courage you need. Philippians 4:13 reminds us, "I can do all things through Christ which strengtheneth me." With God's help, you have the power to overcome obstacles, resist temptation, and continue growing in your faith. Challenge yourself to keep seeking God's will in everything you do. Stay dedicated to Him, not just when it's convenient, but every day, in every decision. Surround yourself with people who encourage your faith and push you to be the man God has called you to be. Let your life be a reflection of His love and truth to the world around you.

Now is the time to commit fully to the Lord, giving Him your best and staying determined to follow Him wherever He leads. The path may not always be easy, but the rewards of living a life dedicated to God are far greater than anything the world can offer. Be faithful in the small things, and God will trust you with greater opportunities. Stay in His Word, seek His guidance in prayer, and never stop growing in your relationship with Him. The more you dedicate yourself to God, the stronger your faith will become, and the more you will see His hand at work in your life. Take up the challenge to live with determination and dedication for the Lord, knowing that He will walk with you every step of the way. Let your faith be a light that shines brightly in the world, and remember that the impact of a life fully committed to God can change not only your own future but the lives of those around you. Keep striving, keep believing, and keep building strong faith as a young man dedicated to God's purpose.

Don't miss out!

Visit the website below and you can sign up to receive emails whenever Joshua Rhoades publishes a new book. There's no charge and no obligation.

https://books2read.com/r/B-A-AJLBB-FZLAF

BOOKS 2 READ

Connecting independent readers to independent writers.

Did you love *Determination and Dedication Building Strong Faith As A Young Man*? Then you should read *Courage Under Fire: David's Stand On The Battlefield*[1] by Joshua Rhoades!

Courage Under Fire: David's Stand on the Battlefield" recounts the stirring first-person narrative of David, a young shepherd boy who faced the colossal Philistine warrior, Goliath, armed with nothing but a sling, a few stones, and an unwavering faith in God. My journey begins with my humble obedience to my father, Jesse, who sent me to deliver provisions to my brothers on the front lines. Despite their scoffing and jeers at my presence on the battlefield, I remained undeterred, feeling a deep sense of duty not only to my family but also to the cause they were fighting for. This sense of duty brought me before King Saul, who, upon hearing my bold offer to fight Goliath, expressed severe doubts about my abilities. He looked upon my youthful frame and could not see how I, with no armor or sword, could face such a fearsome giant.Goliath himself, towering and menacing, mocked me as I stepped onto the battlefield,

---

1. https://books2read.com/u/3G7wPP

2. https://books2read.com/u/3G7wPP

his words heavy with contempt and surety of victory. His towering figure clad in armor, with a spear like a weaver's beam, seemed invincible. Yet, as he taunted me, I felt a profound calm settle over me; I knew that the battle was not mine but the Lord's. I declared as much to Goliath, telling him that the God of the armies of Israel whom he had defied would deliver him into my hands. With a simple sling and a stone, and faith as my greatest weapon, I struck the Philistine on his forehead. The giant fell face down to the ground, and I stood over him, a boy no longer underestimated but recognized as the instrument through which God showed His power.This historical moment is not merely a testament to my personal courage but serves as a beacon of inspiration for every Christian facing their own "Goliaths." Whether these giants are doubts, fears, or seemingly insurmountable challenges, the story exemplifies how faith in God equips us to overcome them. The practical lessons derived from this experience emphasize the importance of obedience, humility, and trust in God's power over our own. In moments of trial, we, like I once did, can draw strength from understanding that God's purposes will prevail over our adversities. As I recount my stand on the battlefield, it becomes clear that true victory in life comes from putting our faith into action, trusting in the Lord's guidance, and stepping forward with courage, even when the odds seem overwhelmingly against us.

www.ingramcontent.com/pod-product-compliance
Lightning Source LLC
Chambersburg PA
CBHW022106150726
47990CB00003B/1258